SPANISH RECONQUISTA
RELIGIONS IN BATTLES

HISTORY 6TH GRADE
CHILDREN'S EUROPEAN HISTORY

BABY PROFESSOR
EDUCATION KIDS

Speedy Publishing LLC
40 E. Main St. #1156
Newark, DE 19711
www.speedypublishing.com

In this book, we're going to talk about the Spanish Reconquista. So, let's get right to it!

WHAT WAS THE RECONQUISTA?

The "Reconquista" translated from the Spanish means the reconquest. This span of history lasted about 780 years. It began when the Muslims

THE ARRIVAL OF CHRISTOPHER COLOMBUS TO AMERICA, 1492

conquered Hispania in 711 AD and ended around 1492 AD when Christopher Columbus discovered the Americas. The location was the Iberian Peninsula.

A Map of
SPAIN
& PORTUGAL,
Drawn from the
Best Authorities.
BAY OF BISCAY
FRANCE
GULF OF LYON
ATLANTIC OCEAN
GALICIA
OLD CASTILE
NEW CASTILE
LA MANCHA
GRANADA
MEDITERRANEAN SEA
AFRICA
MAJORCA
MINORCA
GULF OF CADIZ
Straits of Gibraltar
Cape Palos
Barcelona
British Statute Miles
Longitude West from London
Longitude East from London

WHERE IS THE IBERIAN PENINSULA?

The Iberian Peninsula is at the tip of the continent of Europe at its southwestern edge. Today it contains the tiny country of Andorra, as well as Portugal and Spain.

At one time, this peninsula had been a very prosperous section of the mighty Roman Empire.

THE MUSLIM CONQUEST OF SPAIN

After the western section of the Roman Empire collapsed in 476 AD, the Iberian Peninsula underwent a period of instability. A tribe from Germany, called the Visigoths, overran the area and were in power until around 711 AD. At that time, the Arabs who were Muslims and whose religion was Islam started an invasion of the Peninsula.

THE ATTACK OF VISIGOTHS IN ROME

TARIQ

Their leader was Tariq Ibn Ziyad. He and his soldiers began a military campaign to take over the area, which took 7 years. They landed at Gibraltar, which actually comes from the Arabic words for "rock of Tariq."

The conquerors called the peninsula "Al-Andalus." It became the most western section of a huge empire run by the Muslims. Their leaders were called caliphs and the caliphs who were in power were the Umayyad Caliphs. They ruled from the city of Damascus in the country of Syria.

THE ISLAMIC EMPIRES GOLDEN AGE

In the year 750 AD, the Umayyad Caliphs were almost destroyed by a rival group called the Abbasids. The Abbasids had a banquet and invited the Umayyads. However, it was planned as a trap. They began to club the 80 important Umayyad leaders to death before dinner was served. Only one person escaped this bloody scene.

It was Abd Al-Rahman I. He was only 19 years old at the time and the grandson of the caliph who had been the tenth to reign. He leaped out of the banquet hall through

a window. Then, he swam the width of the River Euphrates and escaped in disguise. He was a fugitive for 5 years as he hid from the Abbasids. He traveled to Spain in 755 AD.

There, he established help from supporters so that he could begin another Umayyad reign. His empire in Spain would become as influential as that of his enemies the Abbasids who were the dominant power in the Middle East.

Al-Rahman I founded his capital city and called it Kurtuba, known as Cordoba today. Eventually it became an enormous and prosperous city that was as large as Constantinople, in the Christian empire, and the city of Baghdad, which was a Muslim city in the east.

MOSQUE OF CORDOBA

Al-Rahman's new Umayyad Caliphate was a very tolerant empire. Although the Islamic religion was by far the most dominant, Christian as well as Jewish professionals, such as doctors, artists, architects, and teachers all thrived under their leadership.

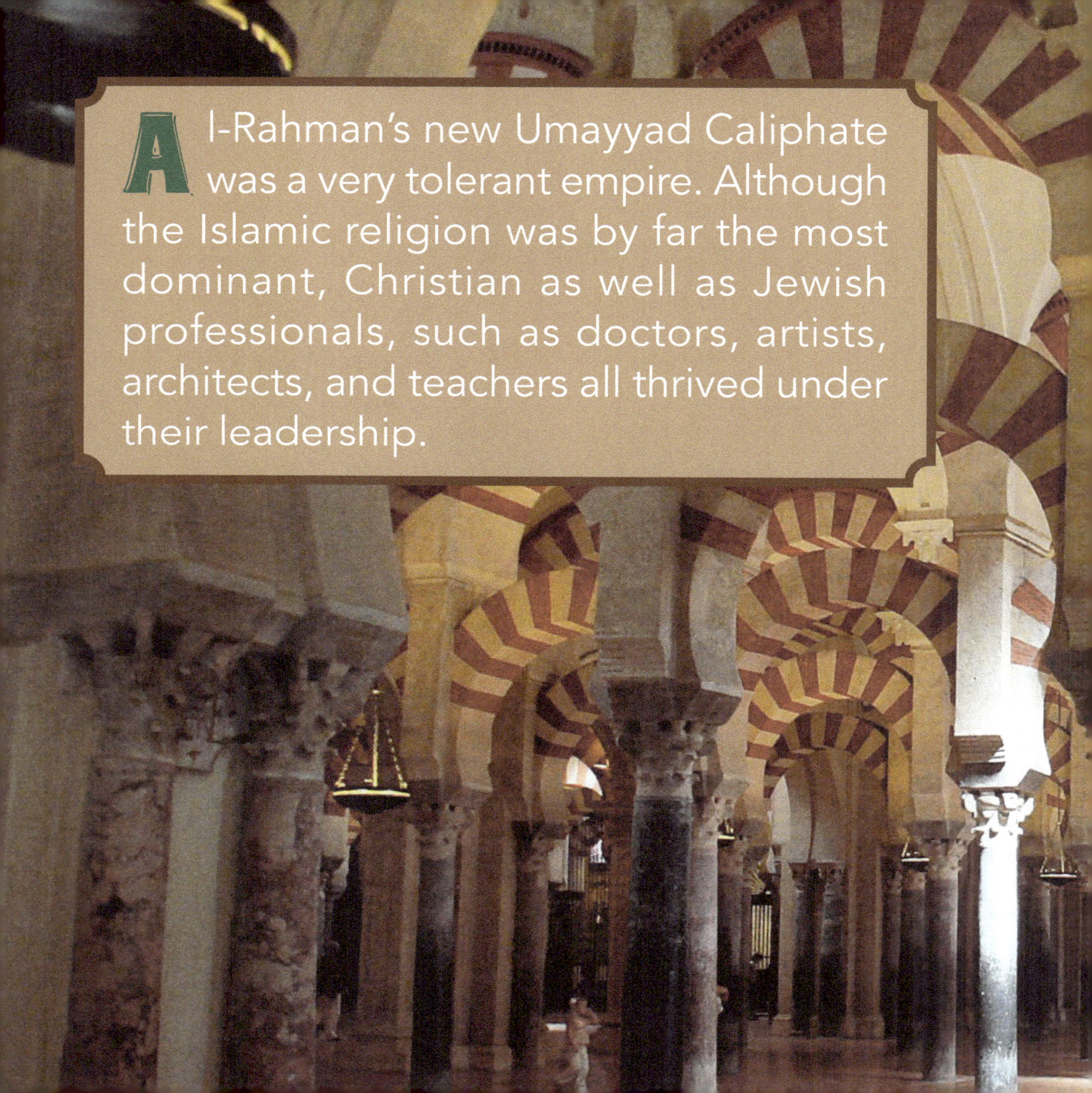

In addition to their tolerance of different faiths, the Umayyads also had a different attitude toward women than many of today's modern Muslim cultures. Women

were allowed to become literate. Quite a few women learned calligraphy and became court scribes.

MUSLIM PRAYING IN A MOSQUE

However, even in this era, certain actions weren't tolerated. If someone committed a blasphemous act, such as any act that was perceived as against God, the person would be killed immediately. Also if a Muslim tried to convert to another religion, he or she would be executed.

The height of the Umayyad Caliphate took place during the years of the Abd Al-Rahman III's reign. He didn't look like most of the other Arab leaders. He had light-colored hair and blue eyes. This was because the caliphs were frequently marrying Basque as well as Germanic wives. Al-Rahman III loved art and architecture. He commanded many beautiful buildings to be constructed.

MADINAT AL-ZAHRA

The library at Cordoba was expanded during his reign. He also built the Madinat Al-Zahra, a huge, majestic palace outside the city. The caliphs had many wives, and Al-Rahman III had this palace constructed for the wife he favored most. Christian visitors to the palace marveled at the incredible treasures that were collected within its walls.

THE CHRISTIAN RECONQUISTA

By 1036 AD, the Umayyad Caliphate began to lose power. In its place several Islamic Kingdoms arose. They were called the Taifas. The Christians began to regain the power they

had had centuries before. They had held a small piece of territory in the northern section of the peninsula. By the late 1080s, they had recaptured many major cities such as Toledo and Madrid.

During this time they had also started some large construction projects as large as the Muslim mosques, such as the beautiful cathedral in Santiago de Compostela, which is designed in the Romanesque style. This cathedral is thought to be the burial place of St. James one of Jesus's twelve apostles.

El Cid, the famous military leader and Christian hero, fought during this era.

There was much infighting between groups of Christians and there were even times when this hero fought for the Muslims against the Christians.

EL CID STATUE

THE ALMORAVIDS

Because the Christians were starting to emerge as a force to be reckoned with, the Muslims from Africa, also called the Moors, were beginning to feel concerned. They were concerned that Islam in the area was getting weak due to corruption and lack of strict observance of the religious laws. The leaders invited a strict Muslim group called the Almoravids to assist them as they fought against the Christians.

The Almoravids were from North Africa. They were fierce warriors and they believed in the literal interpretation of the Islamic holy book called the Koran. They thought that the

Islamic leaders in Spain had become soft in their ways and were actually adopting some aspects of the lifestyle of Christians.

THE ALMOHADS

Of course, because of these differences in thought about the interpretation of Islam, instead of helping the Spanish Islamic leaders the Almoravids decided to take over! They gained power for a short time until an even stricter religious group called the Almohads took power.

MUSLIM WOMAN WEARING VIEL

This group was so strict that they attacked the Almoravid ruler's sister because she wasn't wearing the designated veil that all Muslim women were supposed to wear in public.

JEWS PRAY AT THE WESTERN WALL

The Almohads took over most of the peninsula very quickly, wiping out the Almoravid rule. They stopped the production of wine and they were intolerant of others who wanted to worship differently. They forced Jews and Christians to become Muslims. Many of these people fled to the northern part of the peninsula instead of converting to Islam.

EL REY LOBO

Many of the Muslim people in Spain weren't happy with these new very strict leaders. A soldier named Ibn Mardanis, who was called "El Rey Lobo" or the Wolf King by the people who

were Christians led a fight against the Almohads. Mardanis was a Muslim but he formed a strategic alliance with the Castile Kingdom of Christians to fight against the Almohads.

BATTLE OF LAS NAVAS DE TOLOSA

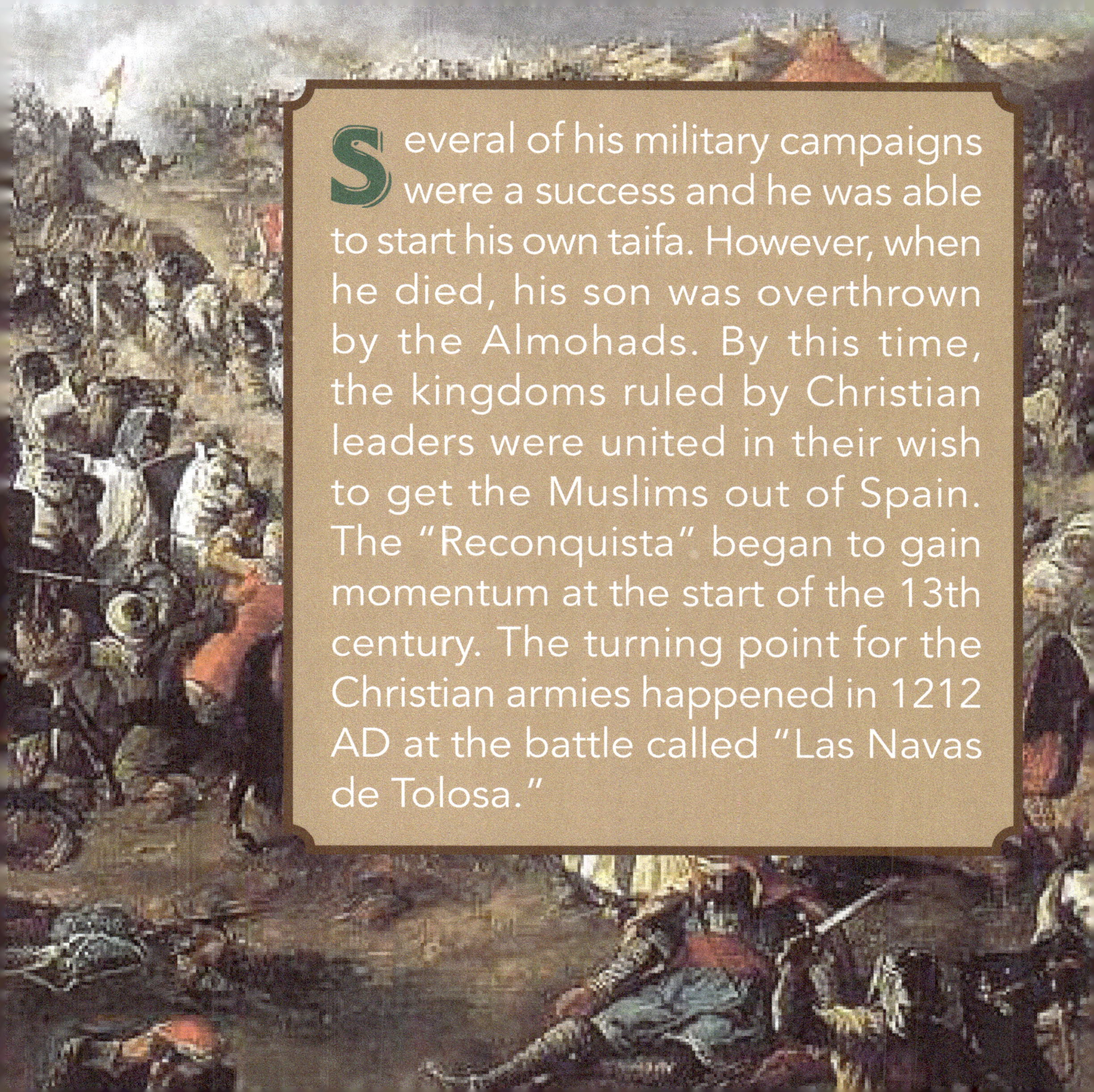

Several of his military campaigns were a success and he was able to start his own taifa. However, when he died, his son was overthrown by the Almohads. By this time, the kingdoms ruled by Christian leaders were united in their wish to get the Muslims out of Spain. The "Reconquista" began to gain momentum at the start of the 13th century. The turning point for the Christian armies happened in 1212 AD at the battle called "Las Navas de Tolosa."

The Christians had put together an army from the region of Castile, the region of Aragon, and the region of Navarre. They also had assistance from France. They defeated the Almohads and soon thereafter other regions, such as Cordoba and Valencia, were overthrown as well. The Christians were back in power after many centuries of Islamic rule. There was only a small kingdom of Muslims in Granada. They were called the Nasrids.

BATTLE OF GRANADA

THE NEW GOLDEN AGE OF SPAIN

The different kingdoms of Christians began to join together into a unified Spanish kingdom. The kingdom of Castile and the kingdom of Leon were joined in 1230 AD. Eventually, in 1474, the

FERDINAND OF ARAGON, ISABELLA OF CASTILE

kingdom of Aragon was added when Aragon's Ferdinand II married Castile's Isabella I. King Ferdinand and Queen Isabella conquered the Nasrids in 1492 and this was the end of Islamic rule in the country.

Despite their Christian beliefs, the king and queen weren't tolerant of Jews or Muslims who were forced to convert or leave the country. They commissioned Columbus to sail for Spain and soon the Christians of Spain would be conquering areas in the New World.

SUMMARY

When the western portion of the Roman Empire collapsed in 476 AD, the Iberian Peninsula was overrun by the Muslims. At the beginning, the rulers were tolerant and allowed others to practice their Jewish or Christian faiths. However, over time, there was a push for stricter adherence of Islamic observances. After 780 years of different forms of Islamic rule, the Christian groups reconquered Spain once more. It was the advent of the new golden age of Spain.

Awesome! Now that you've read about the Spanish Reconquista, you may want to read more about the next era of the Spanish Conquistadors in the Baby Professor book *Did the Spanish Conquistadors Find Wealth and Treasure?*

Printed in the USA
CPSIA information can be obtained
at www.ICGtesting.com
CBHW081204100924
14262CB00067B/51

9 798869 411310